LETTERS TO MOTHER
FROM HARVARD
1937-1938

*Sent by Harry R. Cedergren to his mother, Ellen Stockler, who was living in
Seattle, Washington at the time*

*Compiled and edited by his daughter
Berneal Cedergren Williams
December 2009
Wilbraham, Massachusetts*

Order this book online at www.trafford.com
or email orders@trafford.com

Most Trafford titles are also available at major online book retailers.

Note for Librarians: A cataloguing record for this book is available from Library
and Archives Canada at www.collectionscanada.ca/amicus/index-e.html

Printed in Victoria, BC, Canada.

ISBN: 978-1-4269-2125-4

Library of Congress Control Number: 2009912301

*Our mission is to efficiently provide the world's finest, most comprehensive book publishing
service, enabling every author to experience success. To find out how to publish your book, your
way, and have it available worldwide, visit us online at www.trafford.com*

Trafford rev. 12/16/09

www.trafford.com

North America & international
toll-free: 1 888 232 4444 (USA & Canada)
phone: 250 383 6864 ♦ fax: 812 355 4082

INTRODUCTION

Over the last couple of years I have been going through my father's old correspondence and files and among other things I found a set of letters that he had written to his mother during the year 1937/38 that he spent at Harvard University pursuing a Master's Degree in Soils Mechanics.   Miracle of miracles, not only did she save the letters, but he saved them as well, and I have the originals. I also have many old photos that he took of Cambridge, Boston, and Harvard University.

There is a lot of history in these letters and photos.

Things were not good for our country (or for our world) at that time. The economy was still recovering from the Great Depression, Hitler was on the move in Europe, and life was uncertain. Ellen Lind Cedergren Stockler, my father's mother, was undoubtedly lonely. She was disappointed in her second marriage, her eldest son had joined the military and was gone, her second child, my father, was far away in some strange place called Boston. She did have a younger son by her second husband, Johnnie, who must have given her some comfort, but the thrust of my father's letters to her was an attempt to cheer her up and make her smile.

I find it very amusing that one of his fears that he mentions is of not being able to find a job in his chosen field once he graduates! Based on what I saw when I worked in Residence Life at Boston University, things for college students don't seem to have changed all that much.

My father and his roommate, Lawrence Aller, succeeded in their chosen professions, published, taught, and became somewhat famous. My father left Harvard after one year of graduate work, but Lawrence continued in the School of Astronomy and eventually received his doctorate. When he passed away in the spring of 2003 he was a Professor Emeritus at UCLA.

These letters from my father anticipate none of this. They both were just pursuing subjects that they loved, unsure about the future and what it would bring. They did, however, manage to have a good time in their adopted city.

On a personal note, in spite of what my father said about Lawrence, he married for love and became a devoted family man. I met him years later, in 1960, when he visited us for a few days in Sacramento. I believe he was on the faculty at the University of California at Berkeley at the time. As far as I know, he never married an heiress, but if he did, he didn't use that as an excuse to stop working.

Bellmour, New Jersey
September 16, 1937

Dear Mother,

Last night, after a rather tiresome journey from Chicago, I arrived at Uncle Victor's home in New Jersey. He lives about a mile from the bus line and I was just a little bit tired to begin with, so by the time I had walked to his home I was glad to rest.

Victor looks just about how I expected. He speaks like a "Swede". His wife is a rather nice person; however I think I might not want to live here always. Not because they are not kind, but I think our ways are very different.

Victor lives out in the country - about as far out as we live from town, and about as far to walk. Here, the nights are cool and the days mild, although two weeks ago, it was very hot during the day.

This morning we ate watermelon picked in Victor's garden. Besides watermelons and cantaloupe they raise carrots, corn, grapes, and other products. He has a little house he built himself - about six rooms. They have a bathtub and wash basin in the house, but no toilet, and no running water. They use coal oil for cooking (costs about 80 cents per month), have a furnace in the basement and have electric lights. Their well is just back of the house.

During the winter the temperature goes down to about 20 below, which is fairly cold. Up in Boston, Victor says, the weather stays cold for longer periods of time, but isn't as bad.

Victor's wife is a clean housekeeper. Before each meal she says grace. I'm afraid I slip up in this respect. They have been nice to me - they want me to stay several days, but I think I will leave Saturday morning so that I can spend a day in New York.

Yesterday I spent a few hours in Washington DC. I took a special tour and saw the printing office where money is made, the Smithsonian Institute (a museum), the Congressional Library containing important papers (the original draft of Lincoln's Gettysburg Address, the Constitution of the United States and other papers of importance), the White House and the Capitol Building.

I also visited Philadelphia. It is an old city. The streets are narrow, dirty and crowded. Chicago was clean and not very smoky - not too smoky. At times Chicago is hot, but otherwise it wouldn't be a bad place to live, but I wouldn't care much to stay in Philadelphia.

20 Mellen Street
Cambridge, Massachusetts
September 21, 1937

Dear Mother,

At long last I have arrived at my destination, Cambridge and Harvard University. Bill Shannon (1) and Lawrence Aller (2) met me at the train at South Station in Boston and together we proceeded to Cambridge on the Subway. Leaving my suit-case with Bill, Lawrence and I went out to look at rooms. Nearly everywhere that we inquired rooms were available; however, in a few days, when students begin to arrive, rooms may not be so plentiful.

We found a boarding house about two blocks from Pierce Hall, the building containing the graduate school of Engineering. We are paying three dollars each per week for the room and six dollars a week for six days of meals. Meals are not served at the boarding house on Sunday, so we will have to eat in restaurants on Sundays. Lawrence and I have a room together, which makes it nice. The place where we are staying is a home with four or five rooms that are rented out to students. Our rent pays for clean sheets every week and cleaning of the room as well as heat and light. We won't begin to eat there until tomorrow, Wednesday, so we don't know how the grub will be. The lady seems rather nice, so I think we will make out O.K. In case we don't like the eats, we can eat elsewhere if we desire, so no matter what kind of meals she puts out, I think we can find something to suit us before long. Bill says there is one place (a restaurant) where we can get good food at a reasonable price. I hope our landlady gives us good food, because it will be much handier to eat in the same house where we sleep.

Well, mother dear, how are things in Seattle? Don't worry yourself about me. I will manage somehow, no matter what comes up.

In a few moments I am going out for lunch, so I will sign off now, however I will try to write a long letter in a day or two and let you know more about Cambridge and Harvard.

People around here seem to be rather nice on the whole, so I think we will be contented while we are here.

Say hello to Dad (3) and Johnny (4). Later on I will have plenty of folders and pictures to send him. Love to you, mother dear.

Harry.

20 Mellen Street
Cambridge, Massachusetts
September 23, 1937

Dear Mother,

This is just a short note letting you know that I have had a couple of good nights of sleep, a few good meals, and feel fine.

If everything turns out as well as I think it will, the coming year will be very fine. The people whom I have met at Harvard seem nice. Our room is close to school and the whole set-up looks pretty good to me.

The meals we have had at this place have been very good, so far. I hope they continue to be as good.

When you write, let me know how everything is at home.

Loads of love to you,

Harry

20 Mellen Street
Cambridge, Massachusetts
September 26, 1937

Dear Mother,

If there is anything in particular you want to know about Boston and Harvard, ask me, and I will try to tell you. Lawrence and I are doing fine. We have been company for each other, so we haven't been as lonely as we would be if we had been entirely on our own.

Let me tell you what Lawrence and I did today. We got up at about noon, went out and had lunch, returned and washed our dirty clothes, and wandered about Cambridge for the rest of the day – until dark, I mean. For the last hour or two we have been writing. After school begins we may not have so much time for writing letters, so if you don't hear from me so often, don't be alarmed.

This year should be a valuable experience for me. When I finish I should be able to get a pretty good position.

Mother, remember that I love you and that I think you are the nicest mother anybody ever had. I send you all of my love.

Your son, Harry

20 Mellen Street
Cambridge, Massachusetts
October 15, 1937

Dear Mother,

It's been several days since your last letter arrived. I hope that you are well. You needn't worry about me. So far, I have been feeling fine. We get good meals, and plenty of food, so we probably won't go hungry.

Is dad working steadily? How are things in Seattle? You said that the weather wasn't too good. Well, it is getting a bit cold here. It isn't freezing yet, but we will probably have plenty of cold weather before the winter is over. It's a good thing that we are close to school. As it is, if we put on plenty of clothing before going out the cold doesn't bother us much. I'll write and let you know how we are making out from time to time.

School is well under way, and we all have plenty of work to do. When one is busy he doesn't have time to really get lonely. Sometimes I get just a wee bit homesick, but I am usually busy with something or other that keeps my mind off such things. Well, mother dear, I will say good-bye for now, and wish you the best of everything. Good-bye mother darling, I love you.

Harry

November 4, 1937

Dear Mother,

This will be just a short letter, telling you that I am OK.

The weather has been rather nice for the past month, but nights are brisk. No doubt we will have some cold weather before long. Don't be worried, because I have only two blocks to walk to school.

Say hello to Dad and Johnny. Tell them that I wish I were there to tell them myself.

I have quite a lot of work, but now and then I take an evening off. Lawrence and I have been listening to a Symphony Orchestra Sunday evenings and I have been going to a few dances given by a church a few blocks from here - so we have time out once in a while.

Harry

November 7, 1937

Dear Mother,

Yesterday (Saturday, November 6) I ushered at the Harvard-West Point football game. So, without paying, I was able to see Harvard and Army battle it out. Harvard scored a touchdown within four or five minutes after the beginning. All through the game until about ten minutes before the end, Harvard was ahead. Then Army made a touchdown and the try-for point making the score 7 to 6 in favor of Army (West Point).

A cold wind blew all day Saturday, but it was nice being out-doors all day. I enjoyed it a lot.

This evening I listened to Tchaikovsky's 5th Symphony by the State W.P.A. Orchestra. It was a marvelous concert, worth many times the quarter we paid to hear it. Last night I danced for a while at the Congregational Church around the corner. Everything is so very handy here. One can do anything, and get home in just a few minutes.

Well, mother dear, I hope you are well, and that John and Dad are. Say hello to them for me, won't you?

You mentioned that you may build a house on 35th Avenue. Before doing something like that you should be able to see your way ahead for a little while anyway. With conditions so unsettled these days a little caution wouldn't hurt. Perhaps, before long, I can help you out, but just now - you know how things are.

Its bed-time so I am going to say good-night. Pleasant dreams to you, mother darling.

Harry

November 14, 1937

Dear Mother,

I am going to attempt to describe Harvard and things as I find them in Cambridge in some detail. In the first place—our rooming house might be of interest to you. (5) This house, like most of the houses in Cambridge, is a three-story building, about 50 years old - more maybe. Our room is on the third floor, at the front of the building. Just in front of the house is a huge Elm tree (6), which, when we first arrived here, shaded the house considerably. Now all of the leaves are off, the trees are all completely bare, and our room is a little bit lighter than it was at first. Of course, days are shorter now, and winter seems to be not far off. Since we arrived the weather has been rather pleasant for the most part. Yesterday it rained torrents, and last night it also rained nearly all night, but I think today will be a pleasant day.

Lawrence and I are planning to go to Boston with a young lady who works at the observatory. Before going we have about three hours to make use of (it is now 10 am) so I decided to write to you. We also have to have breakfast, and we have a small washing to do this morning, so we will be occupied most of the day.

To get back to the Elm trees: all of the streets of Cambridge are lined with these trees, some of them as great as 4 feet in diameter, consisting of six or eight trunks coming up at one spot. When we first arrived the streets were very beautiful, and a few weeks go, when the trees were so brilliantly colored, the city was just as beautiful as was the country, but now it is rather gray and barren. Of course we have little time for anything but our work, so these things don't make much difference to us.

Right now, as I am writing, four little birds are sitting on the branches of the tree, just outside of my window. One of them is preening its feathers. Maybe it can't see me through the window. They are so close, I can almost touch them.

I can hear a train going by just a few blocks away. It reminds me of the days Lawrence and I spent on the train coming to Boston. That was some trip, believe me, through the Canadian Rockies, into Chicago and on to Boston.

Now, more about the boarding house. Most of the fellows staying here are law students, as the law school is only two blocks away. If we were staying in some other neighborhood our roommates would probably be Astronomers, Business Administration students or some other variety of student, but I guess we will have to put up with the lawyers. At the table, we often have interesting conversations. Some of the fellows are very interesting. One of the boys nick-named Lawrence, "Astro", because he is studying Astronomy. It makes Lawrence a bit mad, but now everybody calls him "Astro", so he will have to get used to it.

On our floor there are two other fellows besides ourselves. One of them is a third year man in Law. After graduating from some other university, he came to Harvard and is now in his third year. He is "the life of the party" as one of the boys said the other night when he wasn't at the table: "Where is the "Life of the party?" And he really is, he always has something to say. I think he makes believe that he knows more than he really does, but he is an interesting fellow nevertheless. No doubt he thinks Lawrence and I are a couple of barbarians.

Just now, my Egyptian friend, Kamal Khalifa, dropped in. He is a fine fellow, and very interesting to know. Customs in Egypt are in many respects different from those in America and I am enjoying hearing about them. For one thing, they take a nap almost every afternoon - a fine idea!

I have to stop now. Lawrence is at my shoulder telling me that it is time to do our washing, so I will have to quit for the present. I will continue again as soon as I can.

Lawrence is singing the "Apple Polishers song from the Torturette Suite". It goes like this:

"Last night I did Dante read, and he did me so much Intrigue,
I could scarce put the good book down, but cast on me no angry frown
Because I also have my lesson."

Then comes the professor's song:

"Is that so?

A brain-storm I do love to see, but right here between you and me, in this class, some F's there will be."

Then comes the song of the class:

"Sweet Torturettes, how the class loves Torturettes, He gives F's left and right, tho they study all night. Sweet Torturettes, etc. etc."

It is part of a song Lawrence composed for a school play.

Now I have a few minutes again. In a little while we will go out for breakfast. It is only 15 minutes to 12. We just did our washing. I am ready to go out to eat and Lawrence will be in a minute, so I am afraid I will have to stop now.

The iron burned out. We have got to have it fixed, so we can press our pants and Lawrence can iron his shirts.

One thing we are learning here at Harvard. And that is the art of washing clothes. If we can do nothing else, we will be able to take in washing when we get through here. You should see us, every Sunday morning down in the basement, bending over the tubs. We are planning to take a picture of us hanging out clothes when there is snow on the ground.

I have just had breakfast, and have a few more minutes before it will be time to leave for this girl's place with whom we are going to Boston for a couple of hours. We plan to stop at the Boston Art Museum (7), and possibly some other places.

I was telling you about the fellows at our rooming place. The other fellow on our floor is an Education major. He plans to teach science when he gets through here. I occasionally go out for a walk with him. Sometimes a short Italian boy downstairs goes along. After dark it is rather fun walking down to Harvard Square and back.

One of the fellows who eats at our place, but lives elsewhere, seems to have plenty of money. At least he is always talking of the expensive places he goes to, the high price he pays for Saturday night dinners, etc. He has time to play Bridge several nights a week, and goes out a lot. One of the other fellows who is in his third year at Harvard expressed the opinion that this other fellow would have to watch out. Last year about one-third of the fellows in the Law school flunked out.

In the morning we sometimes have to wait about ten minutes to get into the bathroom to shave. We usually go to bed at about 11:30 and get up at about 8:00 am. Breakfast is served at 8:30 am and classes begin at nine o-clock. We have lunch shortly after 1:00 o'clock and dinner about 6:30 in the evening. Breakfast usually consists of some kind of juice, coffee, toast and cereal. For lunch we often have salads, or a hot plate of some kind, milk, bread, sometimes soup, and some kind of dessert. In the evening we sometimes have soup, a hot plate with meat and vegetables, sometimes chicken, on Friday we have fish, and also milk, bread and butter, and dessert.

Our landlady puts out pretty good meals. I think I am eating almost as well as when I was going to the University of Washington. Of course, we may sometimes not have enough, but we often have more than enough, and the meals are regular. In that respect they are as satisfactory as eating sandwiches for lunch and warmed-over food for supper like I was doing. Don't think I am complaining about the way I was treated at home. Far from that. But I simply want you to know that I am not starving. Many times I wish that I could sit down to one of your meals. But this is no time to get sentimental. I must continue with my descriptions.

Let me tell you more about the house we are living in. It is old, as I mentioned before, but I think it is substantial enough not to blow over in a heavy wind. Altogether there are ten students living here. The stairway is very creaky, and when Lawrence comes down in the morning for breakfast, he shakes the house. He tramps rather heavily, and on the old stairs it makes plenty of noise. Likewise, the boards on the floor of our room squeak. By being careful of the places one steps it is possible to cross the room without creating a noise, but rather difficult. At night, it is rather embarrassing to hear every step setting up a squawking noise.

Our room is rather pleasant. As I have mentioned, it faces the street. It has been just recently papered, and on the whole isn't bad. Our landlady is pleasant, so things could be worse. In fact they could be much worse.

We spent a rather enjoyable afternoon going over to Boston. From this girl's apartment we took a bus to Harvard Square, where we boarded the Subway car for Boston. Street-cars go on the surface here, just as they do in Seattle, but in busy sections they drop below the level of the street. Then there is no traffic to contend with, so they make good time. From Cambridge to Boston it takes about ten minutes on the subway, while the same trip on the street-car requires nearly thirty minutes. The cars in the subway usually run in sections of two or three cars, just like trains. As I suggested, they go rather fast, and make a lot of noise. Since the Charles River separates Cambridge from Boston, the subway comes up for air to cross the river. Then it drops back under the ground again and continues through Boston.

Today we went to Fenway Court to the Gardner Art Museum (8). Just a few minutes after we entered, a concert began, so we listened to it before looking about. It was all free, so you see we weren't spending a lot of money. Why, we even walked back home. Virginia suggested walking. It was about three miles, I would judge, possibly a little more, but not much. At Virginia's place we were treated to tea. From there we walked back to Harvard Square and had a bite to eat. Then we came home. It is now 5 minutes to 7. In about 45 minutes we will go out to hear the symphony at Sander's Theatre (9), which is about a 6 or 7 minute walk from here. These concerts are 25 cents and have been very good, at least the Tchaikovsky part has been good. Last Sunday's concert was especially enjoyable.

In order to be able to write up my notes and reports, I quite naturally need a typewriter. When I told Lawrence that I intended to rent one, he told me that he had one in California, and that he could have it sent to Cambridge. Well, that sounded O.K. to me, so I merely rented one for a period of one month, intending to use his when it arrived, thereby saving about ten dollars. The Coop (10), which is a University controlled store, rents typewriters at the rate of about twelve dollars per school year. I figured that by renting one for a month I would save. Well, when Lawrence's typewriter came, it turned out to be a relic. It was a very small portable, about 15 years old, and terribly difficult to operate. After spending about an hour trying to write up my notes I quit. So, in the end, I went back to the Coop, had them get the kind of typewriter I wanted (this one has small type) and rented it for the remainder of the school year. In the end, it cost more than it would have if I had simply rented it from them in the first place, but I didn't know that such would be the case. Of course I am out only three dollars that I paid for the other typewriter for one month, but Lawrence paid several dollars to have the other typewriter sent here from California. The thought never occurred to him that his typewriter wouldn't be good enough. He is like that.

A rather interesting thing occurred in my art class the other day. The Professor had been telling us about paintings and drawings by old Masters, famous painters and draftsmen, and then he produced several dozen drawings by these artists. He explained that this is the only Art School in America where such a thing is possible. In England and Europe it is possible, but to be able to do that in America is something. You see, the art school is located in the Fogg Art Museum (11), which is a famous museum and contains wonderful collections of art.

I am enjoying most of my courses here at Harvard, although it is a lot of work. So far, I am just about managing to keep up with it, but it means that I can't go out much in the evening. That is fortunate in a way, because I haven't much money to spend.

Say, what am I going to do? My socks are beginning to get holey. I will either have to mend them, send them to the laundry, or find somebody to mend them for me. Maybe I could send them to you! I wonder if it would pay. I guess the postage would be rather high, but don't be surprised if you get a big package of socks in the mail some day! Likewise, I may decide to send you a bundle of laundry!

Saturday Lawrence went to the football game. It poured all afternoon, so he came home soaked to the skin.

A couple of weeks ago, we had a heavy rain, which came down on streets which were covered with leaves. It was the first heavy rain for several days so there were plenty of leaves. You can imagine what happened. The leaves were washed down to the drains, where they stopped, and plugged up the drains. For an hour it just poured down, and at the end of that time the streets were literally small lakes. It was amusing.

Lawrence wants to use the typewriter to write a letter so I think I will sign off. This time until the next time. I hope that you are all well. Write and let me know how you all are. Lots of love to you, mother.

Your son,

Harry

November 21, 1937

Well, mother I hear in the news that you have had snow. Not to be out-done by you we are now having some ourselves.

Yesterday I watched the most thrilling foot-ball game I have ever seen. (12) Harvard beat her deadly rival, Yale, by a score of 13 to 6. I believe I mentioned that I ushered at the Harvard-Army game. I also ushered at the Harvard-Yale game yesterday. Ushering consists of standing in the isle, looking at people's tickets to see that they belong in one's aisle, and helping people find their seats. All seats are reserved, selling normally for about $3.85 per seat. Just before a big game like the one yesterday, some speculators buy up a number of seats and sell them for about twenty-five dollars. Some of them probably made a lot of money on yesterday's game. Every seat in the place was taken, and people were paying over three dollars for standing room along the top at the back. Many were no doubt turned away.

Yale was the favorite in yesterday's game, having lost no games this year, while Harvard has lost several. However, Harvard outplayed Yale throughout the game, except for a few minutes when Yale carried the ball down the field for a touch-down in the third period.

After the game ended, a mob stormed down to the field, tore down the goal posts, sang victory songs, cheered, and started marching up the street to Harvard Square. I joined in, and stayed with them till they broke up, which was in about a half hour. Of course, I didn't help tear down the goal posts.

Yesterday it was very cold and damp out in the stadium. During the game, a small amount of snow fell. Everyone felt the cold, including me. Although I didn't get wet through my clothes, I now have a slightly sore throat after so many hours outside. I guess I am lucky, considering everything.

While I was watching the spectacular game yesterday, Lawrence spent the time talking with an heiress - the heiress of the J...... millions. She works at the observatory, for experience, I suppose. Lawrence says: "I'm looking for an heiress, and she'll have to do. When I land her, we won't have to work any more. But if I do, it will be for her money, and for no other reason."

Lawrence and I have been invited to Rev. Harbinson's for Thanksgiving dinner. There will also be "three very nice girls - and their mother" we should have a nice afternoon.

Perhaps I should mention that Marion has practically stopped writing. It has been about three weeks since her last letter. Three thousand miles is a long ways away, and a couple of years is perhaps too long to expect anyone to wait. But there are plenty of nice girls in the world, so perhaps when the time comes there will be someone... For the next year I have things to think about besides women .(13)

Remember, mother darling, that I love you, and want you to be happy. But, whether I will come home to stay after one year at Harvard, I don't yet know. If things turn out well this year, it might be wise to spend a little more time at Harvard. I don't know now what will happen or where I will be this summer. Unless business has completely collapsed next year, I should be able to get work during the summer. Maybe if I want to study next year, I will be able to get help from the university.

How does that sound to you? Tell me what you think of such a thing. Please tell me the next time you write.

For the present, I will again bid you pleasant dreams, and send you wishes for the best of everything.

Your loving son,

Harry

20 Mellen Street
Cambridge, Mass.
December 3, 1937

Dear Mother,

Your letters were very welcome. I am sorry that I told you about having a sore throat if it caused you to worry. It was nothing at all. When I told Lawrence that I had told you about it, he said that he never tells his mother about things like that. She would only make a mountain out of a mole hill. Anyway, I have been feeling OK since getting over that cold but now Lawrence has a sore throat and maybe a cold coming on. I hope he doesn't get laid up. So far, he has just a slightly sore throat, but even that is enough to make one feel punk.

Do you recall my mentioning that Margaret F... was going to go with Lawrence and me to Boston to the Museum? It turns out Lawrence won't be able to go Sunday, so I guess I will have to take care of her myself. I just now talked with her on the telephone, and arranged to meet her Sunday afternoon. She has a car, so it will be very convenient. We will probably have dinner at her home afterwards.

Yesterday I did a little shopping in Boston. Shopping is a hard job, one that I dislike. After spending a couple of hours without making up my mind about anything I get a bit discouraged. I saw a lovely necktie that I would have liked, but I really don't need a necktie, so I didn't buy it. After spending two hours, I bought one pair of shorts for 33 cents, and then bought a pair of pants. I am not sure that they are just what I want, but I paid only five dollars for them, so I won't be out much if they turn out to be punk.

The weather here is getting colder. Pretty soon I will have to get a heavy overcoat, so I think I will not buy a suit for the present. Of the two I need a coat more and I can hardly get both now.

If I come back here next year, or go somewhere in the East to work, I will come home next summer if it is at all possible. Please don't think too much about what may happen next summer. It is hard to plan ahead. At least for me it is. I want to do the thing that will be best in the long run, not merely what I would like to do now.

Say hello to Johnny and Dad for me. You might tell Johnny that I won't be able to get him much for Christmas, but I have something in mind that I think he will like. It won't be much, but I am sure he will like it.

Your loving son,

Harry

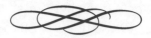

December 12, 1937

Dear Mother,

In my last letter I mentioned that I was going to spend Sunday afternoon in Boston with Margaret F.... We went over to Boston, saw the ski tournament, and then went to the F...'s home for the evening. Today (Sunday) Lawrence and I are going to the Art Museum in Boston (7) with Margaret and maybe one of her sisters.

You might be interested in a brief weather report. For the past week the temperature has been down below freezing. Most of the small ponds are frozen over, the Charles River is beginning to freeze - in short, and winter is just about here. They say that it begins to thaw out sometime in March or even as late as May. Then it gets hotter than h---. So you see, the weather in this part of the country is not as moderate as it is in Seattle. But, for all that, this place isn't bad, except perhaps for short periods when the temperature is down to about 10 degrees below zero and during the summer for a couple of months when it is dreadfully hot. It is fortunate that we have only two blocks to walk to school. If we had a long distance to walk it might be uncomfortable. As it is, the weather doesn't bother us much.

Last week, Lawrence crammed for an examination which he took yesterday (Saturday). It was a terrible examination, very difficult, given primarily for students who have been working for their doctor's degree. Most of those taking it have spent years in the field of Astronomy so they are expected to have considerable background in their field. The night before the examination I bought a bottle of wine, and we each had a couple of glasses. Lawrence asked me to tell you how I got him drunk the night before the examination, so I am telling you about it. He didn't get drunk, however. In fact, he took two or three glasses without showing any effects whatsoever, so he cannot use that as an excuse if he did poorly on the exam.

This morning we woke up at 10:00 am, put our clothes to soak, and had breakfast at the "Coffee Shop", an eating place about two blocks from here. We now have a little time before going down in the basement to wash our clothes. Every Sunday we spend about an hour doing our weekly wash. As I have indicated before, we are becoming expert launderers.

Lawrence has had some interesting, not so pleasant, experiences with his class at Radcliff College where he acts as assistant to Professor Menzel. After he had given the girls an examination, one of them, the "Dizzy Blonde" as Lawrence calls her, saw him on the street, turned her big blue eyes up to him and asked, "Mr. Aller, how did I do in the examination?" Lawrence replied, "Miss R…., how could you do so poorly. You only got one point above class average. I expected you to do much more. And furthermore your grammar was atrocious. You know how fussy Dr. Menzel is on the subject." Then the Dizzy Blond said, "How did Miss A…. do?" Lawrence said, "She did even worse than you did."

A few days later stories of his cruelty reached Lawrence from various people in the observatory. He needs to learn to use some tact with his students. He speaks of "The Dizzy Blond" as a "poor pathetic, cigarette-smoking, tinted clawed, apple polishing, cute little thing".

Another time Lawrence asked Miss R…. why she hadn't come around for night work observation at the astronomy observatory. She said, "Mr. Aller, you have no idea how busy I have been with choral practice and my play". It gets Lawrence down that the girls will play around when they should be working.

Lawrence asked me to tell you that he is trying to save my soul. Incidentally, he has never been inside of a church in his life.

Your loving son,

Harry

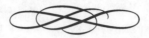

December 26, 1937

Dear Mother,

I have just returned from the Boston Art Museum (7) after spending four hours there. You cannot imagine the marvelous collections on exhibition in the Museum in Boston. Johnny might be interested in knowing that the original paintings of George and Martha Washington by Gilbert Stuart (14) are there, and that there is a painting of Ben Franklin. There are also countless paintings of other important people of those times.

A painting by Turner (15), called "The Slave Ship" is rather famous. This picture shows arms and legs sticking out of the water as people are drowning near the boat. Painted in brilliant tones it is a wonderful picture. Another by John Singleton Copley (16), called "The Woman and the Shark", shows a woman about to be gobbled up by a man-eating shark, while a seaman in a row-boat stands by with a hook trying to spear the shark. One painting by Copley of a young boy is particularly good in my estimation. The young boy in this painting has a fine expression on his face and about his mouth, and his hair, of dark brown, is very lovely. Copley, an American painter, was one of the best of his time, which was about 200 years ago.

In addition to paintings by Americans there are masterpieces by many painters of other nationalities and times. There are two paintings by Rembrandt, which are of course very valuable. Also, there is a wonderful painting, perhaps the best and most valuable in the museum, "Man and his Wife" by Rubens. This picture shows a young woman with her husband standing beside her. She is the dominating figure of the composition. Her face is one that you can't just look at and forget. There is something firm about her lips that holds you. And this picture is marvelously painted. Truly it is wonderful. A guard told me that it was worth nearly a million dollars, so you see -

You may not know it, but many centuries ago artists in Persia, India, China and Japan, in addition to European countries, were producing marvelous works of art. In my art class we have been studying Japanese and Chinese painting. Most of this work is different from the kind of painting one usually thinks of, in fact, you might not even call some of it painting at all. Much of it is what is known as pure delineation, or line representation. By the use of line only the fullness of a face, or the form of muscles on the back of an athlete may be expressed in a marvelously natural manner, and in the representation of trees, grass and bushes a few definite strokes often give the effect of nature. The picture "Bamboo in the Wind" is a good example of this style of Chinese painting.

In addition to painting secular or worldly objects, the Orientals painted many pictures and carved many statues to represent their Buddhas or gods. This type of painting is about the best one can find, and the Art museum in Boston has the best collection of Chinese paintings in the world - or so I am told.

Today I spent four hours in the museum, and then only left because the place was being closed up for the day. One can just spend hours and hours in such a place. It would be a shame to entirely pass up such a marvelous opportunity. Of course there are fine museums in other cities, but the Boston museum is one of the best.

The museum has one of the largest collections of Greek vases in existence. These vases, made about 500 BC or over 2400 years ago, were decorated with human figures, many of them in strange poses. Their purpose was to use the human figure as they saw fit, the object being a pleasing design. The enclosed postcard of the Greek Vase is typical of this kind of work. If you study it closely, you may observe the care and accuracy used in working out the design. The figures are very well made.

A couple of hundred years ago the Indians and Persians were painting highly detailed, tiny miniature portraits. These figures were often only a few inches high, heads being only a fraction of an inch high. In spite of their tiny size, these portraits show a wonderful amount of character and expression. One wonders how it was humanly possible to make them so fine.

In addition to many collections of paintings, furniture, ship models, medals, coins, and a great variety of other interesting things, the museum contains a collection of ancient Greek sculpture. These statues show athletes in action, women, men, and gods in various poses. This work is wonderful. The form of the bodies appears as real as though one were observing the live model.

I could go on and on about the museum, but I must tell you about Christmas as we spent it.

Christmas Eve Lawrence and I were invited to the home of Dr. Menzel (17), one of Lawrence's Professors, or rather, his only professor at the present. After a buffet supper and a couple of glasses of wine, we sang Christmas Carols, while one of the men, a Mr. C…, played the piano. After every other verse Mr. C… played the chords for "A-men", which amused us all. Besides Lawrence, me, and the Menzel family (Dr. and Mrs. Menzel and their two young daughters) a number of friends of the family and people from the observatory were present. After singing carols for the better part of an hour, we played cards for a while. The party broke up rather early, and we got home about 11 o-clock.

Christmas day I was invited to the home of Mr. More, a practicing engineer in this district. Mr. More's work is with a pile driving outfit. Just what his capacity is I don't know. Well, Dr. Casagrande, our professor in soil mechanics, drove two other students and myself out to the More's home in Waban, a part of Newton, which is located about 8 miles west of Boston, and is one of the better residential towns near Boston. Waban is about 3 miles from Wellesley, where the college of the same name is located. Wellesley is about the nicest, snootiest, residential town around here.

Mrs. More was a lot of fun. She has a sense of humor, and made us all feel at home. About 3 pm we sat down to the finest meal we have had since arriving in Boston, maybe with the exception of the Thanksgiving meal at the Reverend Harbinson's at Wakefield. In addition to turkey, we were served baked ham and scalloped oysters, sweet potatoes decked with roasted almonds, a bit of macaroni, dressing, and vegetables. All of this filled our plates to capacity. Before dinner, we all had a drink of brandy in egg-nog, which was very smooth and good, but just slightly powerful, so we all did justice to the dinner. After laying the above-mentioned heaping plate of food away, we also stored away a salad, and then rested while the table was cleared and the dessert, a pudding with brandy sauce, was placed before us. At first I told Mrs. More that I didn't care for dessert, but in the end I weakened and had a dish of pudding with the rest of them.

Mrs. More said that I had smelled the brandy, and for that reason I wouldn't pass it up. Be that as it may, I stayed with the meal to the bitter end.

After dinner, we retired to the living room, and rested, and talked, and played games. Old men got down on the floor beside young kids to play and we all had a lot of fun. During the afternoon and evening about 20 people were there for at least part of the time. Dr. Casagrande left early to go to his daughter's home, but more people came in later, so we had a grand time. After playing games for some time, we had tea and cake. We relaxed for a while and then were taken home.

January 2, 1938

Dear Mother,

I want to tell you about something that happened yesterday which may amuse you. Yesterday, New Year's Day, I met Dr. Shapley, head of the Harvard College Observatory and Astronomical Department, and a number of other people from that department. New Year's Eve I had gone to a dance in Boston and got to bed about 2 o'clock in the morning. The next morning, New Year's Day, I didn't bother to shave, because I planned to do nothing but study. Lawrence had been invited to a tea which was to take place in the afternoon, and so about 4 o'clock, when Lawrence got ready to go to the tea I put on my Lumberjack shirt and my shoes with the hobnails, and went out into the snow with Lawrence, he going to the tea, and I merely going along part way for the exercise.

Nearly a foot of snow lay on the ground and we enjoyed tramping through it. Several blocks from the home of Mr. Campbell, who was host for the afternoon tea, we met several other people who were headed for the Campbell home. Dr. Menzel's two young daughters were there in the care of a young lady employed by the observatory. Since this young woman was planning to not go in to the tea I decided that I would go along as far as the Campbell residence just for the fun of tramping with them in the snow.

Dr. Menzel's daughters (7 and 9 years old, respectively) are two swell little girls. We had a lot of fun throwing snow at each other and pushing each other into the snow. Well, when we arrived at the Campbell's everybody went in, including the young woman who hadn't planned to go in, so I was obliged to follow, dressed as I was. Several of those who had been invited (I had not even been invited) were wearing ski clothing, so I wasn't entirely alone with my rough costume. I was the only one present, however, who needed a shave.

Most of the important folks on the observatory staff were present, so now they know who is responsible for the barbarism Lawrence occasionally displays. When I was introduced to Dr. Shapley he said, "Oh, you are Lawrence's roommate, are you not?" He was very pleasant, however, and I enjoyed talking with him. During the time we were there, we talked with the young men and women, and with some of the older folks, had tea and sandwiches and other goodies, and then listened to part of the football game at the Rose Bowl in Pasadena, California.

When tea was prepared, we were told that we would have to serve ourselves, so I started to walk across the hard-wood floor of the dining room, being careful not to get the hob-nails on the floor. Mr. Campbell told me, when I explained to him that the soles of my shoes were covered with nails, and that if I sat down tea would be brought to me. So I sat down and my tea was served to me. So, you see, there was an advantage in coming dressed for the woods after all.

Well, mother, my vacation is nearly over. Tomorrow school begins in earnest again. Then in about a month this term will be over, and another will begin.

Before going back to work I am going to lie down for a few minutes, so I will stop now. I will take this opportunity to wish you and the rest of the folks a Happy New Year! I hope it will be a happy year for all of you. Also I send you my love, mother dear. And once again - sweet dreams....

Your loving son,

Harry

January 29, 1938

Dear Mother,

For the present I am a man of leisure. Yesterday I took my last examination, so I am now free until classes begin again next semester. This will be on Monday, February 7, so I have over a week in which to rest up for the second half of this year at Harvard.

I am glad to have the examinations over. Some of them were rather long, and for that reason, difficult to finish in the time allowed (three hours). In fact, our professor in Structures allowed us an extra ¾ hour, and I still didn't finish. Nearly everyone else was in the same fix, however, so I think I made out all right. Whether I will get any A's or not I do not know, but I am fairly confident that I will pass all of my courses.

The last couple of nights were rather cold. Lawrence and I were out for a short walk and observed that the thermometer was at 22 degrees. Of course that isn't as cold as it gets, but it was fairly cool. Maybe we are in for some more snow; at least the sky looks threatening. That would make Lawrence happy. On Sunday nights that are clear he has to work all night running telescopes at the observatory.

It seems that the director of the observatory has allowed plenty of money for photographic plates but none for a night assistant on the night the regular man has off, which is Sunday. Consequently, someone has to do the job, and without pay, so students are appointed for a period of about 5 months each. Lawrence has just been given his turn, much to his dislike. He has more work to do now than should be expected of anyone, and on top of that, he now has to put in about 14 hours on Sunday nights, doing a dull job for no pay. Of course, that makes a wreck of him the next day, but that's just part of the game, I guess. Fortunately, nothing like that takes place in the Graduate School of Engineering.

Well I don't know what else to say, so I will go out and mail this letter and then maybe walk around Cambridge for a while and then come home, and get ready for supper. This evening I am planning to go to a dance given by the church up the street. Admission to their dances is only 25 cents, so it isn't a very great extravagance. The people are rather nice, so when I am not too busy I like to go.

So long.

Your loving son,

Harry

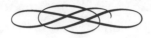

February 3, 1938

Dear Mother,

I guess I don't need to tell you that I am looking for those cookies. When they get here we'll have to watch our step or we will eat ourselves sick. For Christmas, Lawrence's sister sent him a lovely fruit cake which we have finally disposed of, so we can now make good use of a few home-made cookies.

Today is Thursday. Next Monday classes begin again, so I am just loafing this week. Time certainly flies, but on the other hand, it seems a long time since we took that summer boat-ride to Victoria. I just wrote a letter to Minnie D..., the University of Washington girl we had out for dinner one evening before school finished last year, and told her of our trip East. My letter was in reply to a letter that she had written to me. I told her of meeting Lawrence at the train station in Vancouver, and of the way he was loaded down with a pillow, my raincoat under one arm, bags of fruit, fish, etc. under the other; how my raincoat got dragged through the mud of Chicago, Duluth, and a number of other cities. It was a brief description of the entire trip, from Seattle, through the Rocky Mountains, and here to Boston.

Tonight Lawrence is out at a party given by the Astronomy people, so I am here by myself. Of course, Lawrence nearly always studies at the Observatory in the evening, so this is no different from usual. Last night I went over to Boston to see what was going on.

I was tired today, so I went to bed after lunch and slept an hour or two. Now I feel fine. Kamal, my friend from Egypt, takes a nap every afternoon. That is a national custom in Egypt. In that country the people seem to be in less of a hurry than we are in America. He commented on this difference one of the first times that I talked with him.

This evening it is raining. Just a short while ago I returned from a walk around Cambridge. Earlier today I walked down by Central Square, one of the business districts of Cambridge, which is supposed to be a more or less tough district, although I saw no evidence of anything different from any other business district in Cambridge or Seattle, for that matter. Evidently the evening rush was on, because the street was jammed with people hurrying to and fro.

Walking along Massachusetts Avenue one now and then hears the rumble of a street-car, although no car is in sight. If you don't know of the existence of the subway, this noise is mysterious. Even when you know that the train is passing under you, it seems a bit odd.

Nevertheless, the subway system has advantages over surface trolleys. Right through the center of town the street cars go just as fast as out in the sticks. As long as one wants to go somewhere near the subway, he can do so very quickly, but if his path does not lie near the subway, then he can spend an hour to go just a few miles. Often it is just as quick to walk as to go by the circuitous round-about way the elevated goes. One day Lawrence and I went to Boston with the Mink, a girl I have spoken of before, and walked back to Cambridge from the Art museum. Actually, I was surprised at the short distance we walked. At the most it was three or four miles.

Well, now it is Friday morning. I am going to write several more letters today, so I will stop now. Once more I send you all my love.

Your son,

Harry

February 6, 1938

Dear Mother,

Your cookies arrived the other day, and they are swell. I gave a couple of them to two of the boys living on our floor and they both commented on how good they were. We have eaten about half of them and the rest will be gone before long.

Tomorrow, classes begin again. Soon the second half of this year will be well under way.

Last night I went to a burlesque show with one of the boys who eats here. Principally, the program consisted of dance numbers by a group of nearly nude female dancers, with time out occasionally for jokes by a couple of males. The primary concern of the dancers was to show as much of their bodies as possible. During the few times that they wore anything besides the little strip around their body they were careful to expose themselves as frequently as possible.

One of the most popular dancers, a rather fat creature, did all sorts of crazy things. She turned her back to the audience and shook her a--, then she shook her breasts. Another of the dancers was rather graceful and had a very pleasant smile. None of them could sing worth a d---, they danced very poorly, but I will admit they knew how to show themselves off. The fellow with whom I went goes there now and then. Personally, I don't care to ever see that kind of show again. I hope it doesn't leave a bad taste in one's mouth.

Today Lawrence and I went for a walk down beyond the Charles River. Just a few blocks from Harvard are filthy hovels where the poorer people of Boston live. This place would surprise you. Within just a block or two one sees the finest places there are, and the worst. Returning to the Harvard (Cambridge) side of the River, we walked past

Dunster House, one of the most elegant student houses. To see what kind of conditions we might find, we walked up the street back of Dunster House. Some of the worst dumps in Cambridge, I think, are on that street. On one side of the street is this fine, brick building, in which students in Harvard College live. On the other side of the street are houses which ought to have been torn down years ago. One of them has its windows boarded up. Dirt and filth lie about them all. A block up this street we passed four young fellows, evidently natives of Cambridge and of this particular area. As we passed, they made bright cracks, and continued to hurl spiteful remarks at us until we were far up the street.

On the Boston side of the Charles River we came upon a street called "Seattle Street". Since it was in a rather dirty district I was not complimented, but it was nice to see that name, even there. (18)

Lately I have been going to church Sunday evenings. There is a church a few blocks from here which I have told you about before, the Methodist-Episcopal Church. The people who go there seem to be very nice. Perhaps my main reason for going is to be able to mix with these people. Anyway, it is a very pleasant way to spend Sunday evenings. After the meeting, they sing songs or play games - and serve tea and cookies. Johnny would probably like that part.

Well, Mother, it is now 10 minutes past seven. Church begins at 7:30, so I will sign off now.

Remember, pleasant dreams mother dear.

Your loving son,

Harry

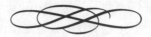

February 14, 1938

Dear Mother,

Your letter (and John's) just arrived. I have been looking for a letter from you, so I was glad to see it on the table downstairs when I came in this evening.

Today I have been out buying some things for an experiment I will be doing in a research course I am taking. The University pays for the equipment, but I have the job of determining the procedure. It shouldn't be too difficult, and once I get the apparatus set up it should be rather interesting work.

Last semester I got one A and four B's in my courses. The Art course took so much time that I dropped it at the end of the first semester. Also, I decided to drop a course in Structural Theory and enroll in one more in Soil Mechanics. Now I am taking just four courses, and auditing one, so I should have little difficulty keeping up with everything. Out here they want you to work your head off, and Dean W...... seemed to not like the idea of my dropping his course. Anyway, I want to do as well as possible in the courses I do take.

Johnny asked if we have had snow, or rather if we have any. Just now there is no snow on the ground, but we have had about 18 inches of snow this winter. A normal winter's snow here is about 40 inches. This winter, they say, has been mild. I would hate to spend a normal winter in Boston!

Last week Lawrence and I went to two concerts which were free. One was given by Harvard and the other by Radcliffe, which is the women's school that is affiliated with Harvard.

Lawrence wants to go back to work, so I think I will walk up towards the Observatory with him. Then I have certain work to do for a while this evening.

In a short while I will write you a longer letter telling about things here in Cambridge. All I can tell you, mother, dear, is that I love you dearly and send you my sincerest wishes for happiness.

Your loving son,

Harry

February 17, 1938

Dear Mother,

In my last letter I told you about changing my courses this semester, and that I am only taking four courses. I didn't tell you, however, that all of the courses I am now taking are in Soil Mechanics under Dr. Casagrande. A few days ago, Dr. Casagrande discussed a certain phase of our work in which different investigators have different opinions concerning the proper procedure needed to obtain accurate results. Actually, the differences are not great and Dr. Casagrande mentioned that sometime when he had nothing else to do he would publish the truth about the matter.

A short time later I asked him if a student (meaning myself) could be of sufficient assistance to him to make it worth while to do something about this job. He said that a student could do very little, but suggested that I could get information that had been obtained by another professor, to prove that he, Dr. Casagrande, is right. So now I have obtained this information and am going to see what I can figure out from it. If I were taking five courses instead of four, I would be afraid to take time out for something like this, but now I don't mind. Anyway, it is something I want to know, so it should be time well spent.

Today some equipment came for the research problem I am working on. Now I need to make some drawings for the shop man so that he can do the necessary work.

Lawrence has been suffering from neuritis which has settled in his jaw. At times it bothers him very much. With all the work he has to do, and now neuritis, it's a wonder that he can keep up with everything. Incidentally, he is getting straight A's in his school-work.

Although there is no snow on the ground, spring is still a long way off by the feel of things. In the evening the temperature goes down to about 15 or 20, which is pretty cool.

Often Lawrence and I go for walks around Cambridge. Here there are no small streams to walk beside, and no country roads to walk along, but still, some of the walks in Cambridge are as muddy as the roads on the outskirts of Seattle. Right now, when we wish to take a walk, we just walk around Cambridge. Perhaps when the weather gets more comfortable, we shall go out in the country, but that will be at least a few weeks yet. Maybe when the weather does get warm we will wish it were winter again. If it were not for the extremes in weather conditions this part of the country would be an enjoyable place to live in.

Your loving son,

Harry

February 23, 1938

Dear Mother,

Today I received your letter asking me to send you an airmail letter. I'm sorry it takes so long for you to get my letters, but you must realize that it requires about 5 days for a letter to go one way, and that the soonest ordinary mail can go two ways is about 10 days. Please don't worry if you don't hear from me as often as you like as I may let a few more days pass than I intend between letters.

Last evening, I helped Lawrence and the rest of the Observatory staff assemble pages for a book they are putting out. To save money, Dr. Shapley had the material printed on a Mimeograph machine. To put the pages together requires considerable work, so the entire staff went to work on it for about 2 hours last evening. After the work was completed they had cookies and tea, but I left before that time, so I missed out on the refreshments.

The past two Saturday afternoons, Lawrence and I have listened to a broadcast of the Metropolitan Opera Company from New York. An instructor at Harvard invited Lawrence and me to his home for the afternoon, one week ago last Saturday, and asked us to come every Saturday so long as the operas continue. Both of the last two Saturday afternoons were very enjoyably spent by us. These people, the D..., are very pleasant, and they also invite a number of other people over to listen, so they have a very pleasant afternoon gathering. When the opera is over, they serve a buffet supper. Last Saturday, after the opera, Lohengrin, we listened to a symphony by Beethoven from recordings. The opera, Lohengrin, was very enjoyable. By means of musical devices, Wagner gives very definite moods and very different feelings. For example, to give a feeling of the plotting and scheming that was going on in the minds of two actors, the orchestra played in low, sinister tones - very eerie.

Not only do the D….. have a very fine radio with phonograph attachment, but they have some wonderful books. Last Saturday, I spent about an hour looking through one book showing the paintings of Rembrandt. More than 500 paintings were reproduced in this one book.

Saturday there were two Radcliffe girls there besides Mr. And Mrs. D…, Lawrence and myself. These two women are studying Geology and Zoology, respectively.

Johnny might be interested in knowing that we had another five or six inches of snow the other night. Most of it has melted, however, since it is rather warm out just now.

Well, mother, I guess I will stop now, and get to work writing up a lecture in Soil Mechanics. When I go out I will drop this letter in the box, so that you will get it as soon as possible.

So long, mother dear.

Harry

February 27, 1938

Dear Mother,

Yesterday Lawrence and I went over to hear the broadcast of Aida at the home of Mr. D….. It so happened that only one other guest besides ourselves was there. After the Opera, we listened to part of a program from Germany on short wave. Almost any time they are able to pick up European broadcasting stations on their radio. Much of the stuff broadcast from Germany is propaganda telling how much conditions have improved in Germany since Hitler took up the reins, that Hitler hasn't got a broken arm like American newspapers have said he has, etc. etc.

Friday evening I went with the Mink to a recital of viola and piano given by Harvard University. After we were seated, we noticed that there was no piano on the stage. I commented on it to the Mink and we decided that evidently it would be brought in very shortly, and that we would see an exhibition of piano moving. Well, about ten minutes after the program should have begun, a gentleman came out on the stage and told us that the last he had heard "the piano was on the way". Since the first number was to be a viola solo, Paul Hindemith, the artist, presently began the first number. After he had finished the announcement was made that the program would be continued in the Music building, which was about two blocks from Sanders Theatre, where we were then sitting.

Everybody made a wild dash for the Music Building, including myself, the Mink, and Dr. S…, a little German-Jew Astronomer. S…., in broken English, said that he would have to write home that Americans have a funny way of doing things.

The program consisted of compositions written by Paul Hindemith, the gentleman who played the viola. His compositions are what are called "modern". It is very much like the stuff Forest wrote. I don't recall whether I told you about one concert we listened to last year by the WPA orchestra in which a number of Forest's was played. Well, anyway, this music is just a lot of noise. Nothing but discords and chaotic passages. There is really nothing about it enjoyable. Some of Hindemith's stuff wasn't quite so terrible as Forest's stuff, but it wasn't much to write home about. Still, he got a big hand. Compared with this modern noise the compositions by some of the 19th century composers are wonderful. In fact they are wonderful, no matter how you look at it.

Well, mother, it is now six minutes past eight. I believe I will go over to the church, so I will have to stop now. This letter is enough to let you know that I am still able to run the typewriter. Remember, mother dear, sweet dreams.

Your loving son,

Harry

March 10, 1938

Dear Mother,

Today the birdies are chirping in the tree outside. Although it is a bit cool the weather is much milder than it has been for several months. I certainly hope that we will have no more snow. It has been cold and miserable for so long that we have become pretty much accustomed to it all by now. I don't know what I would have done without that wonderful woolen scarf you let me have. At times Lawrence has worn it and he says he doesn't know what he is going to do next winter when he won't be able to borrow it. On cold days it is very comforting to have such a warm garment wrapped around one's neck. You have no idea the comfort it has been - both to Lawrence and me.

Lawrence says that he will miss me on Sunday mornings, next year. He will just have to find someone else to wash clothes with him!

Next summer Lawrence is planning on going to California to work at Lick Observatory on Mt. Hamilton (19). A few days ago he received word that he had been awarded a scholarship of $750 for next year. Now, he is waiting to figure out how he will be able to earn $300 to pay the rest of his expenses. Doing that may prove to be quite a job. This year he has been assisting Dr. Menzel teach a class at Radcliffe. Next year he may have to count stars or spend all clear nights observing. At any rate, he will probably find a way to earn that 300 dollars. During the summer he will spend what he needs to pay living expenses and railroad fare to California and back but that will probably be all. He needs to save as much as he can.

If we can arrange to leave here at the same time, Lawrence and I will try to travel together for at least part of the distance West. As I have said before, I do not know definitely what I will be doing after school is over this year. If I can possibly do it I want to come home for at least part of the summer. I have to try to get a position, so that I can at least pay back what I have been borrowing this year, so my plans depend upon what turns up in the way of a job.

Tell me what you think about this. I would like to know what you really think. For a time it may be necessary to take a position here in the East somewhere, but then later I should be able to find something worthwhile near Seattle. At least I hope so. Do you think that is a good idea?

I have another story to tell about Lawrence. Did I tell you that he asked me to ask Uncle Vic for more of those religious pamphlets that he sent me? Well, Uncle Vic, or his wife, rather, sent me a few religious pamphlets along with a Christmas Card. Lawrence thought they were very funny and wanted some to give his atheistic friends just for a joke. Of course he doesn't believe in religion and most of his friends do not either, but he wanted to pass out some of these pamphlets just to amuse himself and his friends. So, I asked Uncle Victor to send me a few of them - and he did. In fact he sent a whole wad of them. Now Lawrence has a good supply. Victor's wife said "may the Lord bless him as he passes them out". I wonder what she would say if she knew his real purpose.

One thing bothers me a little - but not as much now as it used to. Lawrence used to keep me awake in the evening a little bit later than I like to go to bed. Now we have become more accustomed to living together, so we don't disturb each other much, and we are better off than we were at first. Although Lawrence has an enormous amount of work to do, he comes home in time so that we are in bed about 11:30. We get up in the morning at 8:30, so you see we get plenty of sleep.

Our landlady has been feeding us rather well. For breakfast we have cream-of-wheat with milk, fruit or fruit juice, toast (3 slices) and coffee. At noon we have either a cold plate or a hot plate of some kind with meat, vegetable and potatoes, bread and butter, milk and a dessert. In the evening we have soup, a hot plate of meat, vegetables and perhaps spuds, Jell-O or pie or some other kind of dessert, bread and butter, and milk. Sometimes in the evening we have more than we want, but lunches are rather light. All-in-all we have no kick coming as far as the grub is concerned. In restaurants, meals come higher than Mrs. Ambler's price to us. She puts out well-balanced meals, so I think we are pretty well off in this respect. At least, we don't get tired of her cooking - it is home cooking, which is more than you can say for most of the stuff put out by restaurants. Sunday evenings Lawrence and I go down to Jim's Place, a beer joint down beyond Harvard Square, where we get a meal for 40 cents. We get soup, a plate of some kind - there is very little choice - milk and pie or chocolate cake and ice cream. Except that their menu never changes this place is pretty good. Their food gets tiresome, however, even though we eat only one meal per week. I forgot to mention that we also have bread and butter.

One waitress has been waiting on us ever since we first went there. She brings us a plate of bread and two slabs of butter each when we first sit down. Before we finish she brings another three or four slices of bread and several more slabs of butter. Lawrence likes to fill himself and he usually does - on bread. When we leave this place we are always filled up to the brim.

Last night I looked at the menu in front of the Commander Hotel Restaurant. It is a very ritzy place and are the prices ritzy! Planked steak for two is $4.00. Coffee is 20 cents and milk 15 cents. Sandwiches average about 40 cents. Salads run near $1.00. The minimum price for a meal is about $1.50 more or less. A breakfast of fruit, cream-of-wheat, biscuits and coffee is 85 cents. Their cheapest breakfast is 35 cents which gives the choice of fruit juice or cereal, biscuits and coffee, I think. It must be their special. I don't see how they can afford to give so much for a mere sum of 35 cents. Our landlady figures 20 cents for breakfast. The Commander must be in cahoots with the Canadian Pacific Railroad.

People in these parts like to "put on the dog" as Lawrence says. That is, they pretend they are something that they are not. One of the boys in our house is very conscious of different "strata" or levels of society. Apparently one of the primary bases for judgment is a person's pocketbook. At dances, the fellows buy corsages for $2.50.

Maybe there is really no difference between the East and the West. It may be that we are in contact here with a more "aristocratic" group of people than those we associated with in the West. No doubt the more wealthy people even in Seattle spend more than they should just for the same purpose. Most of my friends, however, could not afford to spend $2.50 for a corsage. I must not forget that we are now at Harvard among the aristocrats. But don't get me wrong. I like Harvard. I'm just giving you some of my impressions.

Last week I spent a few hours working on a job (for which I get paid). Bill Shannon asked me the other day how much time I can put in on this. It pays 80 cents an hour, so I expect to put in a little time now and then during the next couple of months. Maybe I will be able to earn enough so that I can come home on the train instead of on the bus. Traveling on the bus is more tiring than traveling on the train - if one has a sleeper - but if you have no sleeper on the train such a way of traveling is at least as tiring as the bus. As I mentioned some time ago, seats on trains were not built for sleeping. Between Chicago and Philadelphia I tried in vain to find a comfortable position. It was impossible! A couple of the boys here from Washington came on a bus, and it didn't hurt them much, so maybe I will travel that way this summer - if I travel. But, as I said, if I can earn 50 dollars or so, between now and the end of the term I would be able to travel in slightly better style.

This job consists of running tests on soils for foundation purposes. It is very elementary stuff, which requires little knowledge of soil mechanics, but gives experience in running routine tests. This experience may be of some value. The money will come in handy.

When I get home again, will I be able to put on the dog! I can talk about Hawvud (sic) and Boston, New York, Philadelphia, Washington, Chicago, and other places that I have seen. It's too bad I won't be able to go to Europe - this summer, say - then I would really have something to talk about. Coming here to Harvard has given me an opportunity to see a small part of these United States at least. I have now seen the Rocky Mountains you used to tell me about, and I have spent time in New York, which I would never have thought would happen.

One of my classmates is from Oxford University, England. He says that he doesn't plan to stay in one place for a while. There is so much to see, he says, that he can't picture himself staying in one place forever.

Well, I guess I had better stop this rambling. I am not saying anything and I must get back to work. When you write, tell me something about things at home. How is the Governor behaving? Is Snappy still barking at the Moon? How has John been? Is dad putting in a garden yet? And how have you been feeling?

Goodbye mother, dear. I can only send you sincere wishes for your well-being and happiness. And, remember, pleasant dreams, sweet dreams....

Your loving son, Harry

April 24, 1938

Dear Mother,

It is Sunday evening and I have just returned from the church on Massachusetts Avenue. This afternoon Lawrence and I had a rather enjoyable walk with the "Mink" through a cemetery a moderate distance from here (20). After, we had cookies and tea at her house. Lawrence and I then went down to the Square and had our dinner. Just now Lawrence is on duty at the Observatory, waiting until about 11:00 o'clock in the hope that the sky will not clear up before that. If the sky remains overcast, as it is now, he will then come home and go to bed. Should the clouds move on, he will have to work all night, but it now looks hopeful.

This noon, I wrote the following, while waiting for Lawrence:

I am sitting on the fire escape on the side of the observatory. Just now I am waiting for Lawrence, who is having a conference with Dr. Whipple concerning his Thesis. Lawrence's office is just inside the building from where I am sitting, so I will be able to hear him when he returns from his conference. In the meantime I am writing these lines to you.

From my perch up here on the third flight, I can just touch the uppermost branches of an apple tree. On either side other trees form a veil surrounding the observatory and cutting off the view. In a few weeks, when the leaves have developed further, the view will be cut off still more.

Nearly every evening at about 10:30 I drop my studies and march over here to the observatory. At that hour the doors are locked so I climb softly up three flights of fire escape and stand out here until seen by Lawrence. We then go out the front way and start upon our evening walk.

The other evening Lawrence lectured to a group of high school students. Being somewhat bored with my own work I went with him to the observatory. Although I had heard him present a similar talk one time before, I found his lecture rather interesting. Following a discussion about the planets of our own Solar system, he attempted to give the youngsters an idea of the distances between various objects in space.

First, he pointed out, it takes light about one second to reach the earth from the moon. Now, when we remember that light travels at the rate of about 186,000 miles during one second, this distance appears to be rather large. But when we turn our attention to the Sun, the center of the Solar System of which our earth is a part, we see that to reach the earth from the sun, light travels over eight minutes. It is much farther to the Sun than to the Moon. Next, consider the Solar system, which includes the Sun and its planets. Light takes several hours to cross it. You see, we are now getting up into fairly great distances. Five hours or 18 thousand seconds at 186 thousand miles during each second - how far is that?

It's a long way from one end of the Solar system to the other. Such distances are difficult - if even possible - to grasp, although they are still within our own little Solar system. Now, let us look beyond this little cluster of dust spots circling our own Sun, and look toward the nearest star in our Milky Way System. How far is the <u>nearest</u> star? To reach the earth from the nearest star, light requires four years time of continuous travel at the rate of 186 thousand miles per second! It would be meaningless to think in miles. One step farther, we observe that light requires about a thousand years to cross our own Milky Way system of which the Sun is but an average star. How really tremendous this distance is. Let us go a little farther, let us look beyond our Milky Way system. Telescopes have been built which can see entire systems of stars comparable to our own Milky Way, far, far, away from us. Light from these Universes started on its long, long journey millions of years ago. In fact, the largest telescopes see objects from which light has been traveling toward the earth for 500 million years.

Let us summarize. From the moon to the earth: one second. From the sun to the earth: approximately 8 minutes. Across our Milky Way system: 1000 years: From the most distant stars photographed: 500 million years: Some picture, isn't it? Thinking on this scale of distances, 20 Mellen Street is but a step from Seattle - just a step!

After writing the above, Lawrence and I dropped over to the "Mink's" and walked with her over to one of the large "Marble orchards" in these parts. Among other monuments of famous people we saw that of Henry Wadsworth Longfellow. While on the grounds we climbed a tower which is on the highest spot in Cambridge.

Now it is 11:00. If Lawrence doesn't work tonight he will probably be home shortly. Anyway, I am going to bed in a few minutes, so I will sign off.

Again, mother dear, I send you my love.

Harry

May 1, 1938

Dear Mother,

Last evening I had dinner with a family named N… who have an apartment in Boston. Mrs. N…, called "Aunt Polly", appears to be a very cultured lady. Besides Aunt Polly, there was "Aunt Minnie", a somewhat older woman than Polly. Mrs. N… has two daughters: Norma, a student at Radcliffe, and another whose name I can't spell, who is also a student.

A week ago Norma was at the dance at the church around the corner on Massachusetts Avenue, and asked me if I would come to her home for dinner the next Saturday evening. They were having some people who also came from Seattle, and she thought I would like to meet them. I thought that would be nice and told her so. So, last evening, the "Seattle Club of Harvard" had its first meeting at the home of the N…s in Boston.

I was the first of the guests to arrive. After being graciously welcomed by Aunt Polly and Aunt Minnie I was taken into the living room to amuse myself until some of the others arrived. For a few minutes I played recordings on their new radio-phonograph combination. Presently the girls and a few friends arrived. Norma had been doing some research work up at MIT (21) but soon she came home also.

There were two young men, both studying law at Harvard, who had come from Seattle, so we had a few things in common to talk about. I told them of the changes that had been made on the University of Washington campus recently, but soon we were talking about astronomy. Then I told them some of the things I have learned from Lawrence about galaxies and the Milky Way System and such. After several minutes of this, one of the girls asked me if I was an Astronomy Major. I said No, that I was studying Engineering. I explained that my roommate was an Astronomer and that I had learned a few things from him.

Presently we were called into the dining room. Mrs. N… explained that all three of her servants, the maid, the butler, and the cook had left her the same day, so we would have to get along as best we could without them. Of course she was just joking. She teaches, I believe, and her two girls are grown. Aunt Minnie probably takes care of cooking and the rest of the household work. On the table there were four candles burning and the room had little light besides that from the candles, but it was very nice and cozy.

After dinner, we retired to the living room, where we played a few phonograph records, some of them older than I am. After the dishes had been washed and everybody had come into the living room we played a game until 1:30 in the morning. Finally, one of the young men drove me home. He and the other fellow and his wife live in Cambridge anyway, so they didn't have to go out of their way very far.

During the past few weeks Lawrence has given a little German-Jew astronomer, Dr. S…, a number of religious pamphlets of the kind that we got from Uncle Victor. Last night while returning from a night of observing, Dr. S… and Lawrence and several other astronomers were riding together in the observatory car when Dr. S… said: "I wonder who is sending me some crazy religious leaflets all about death, and God and damnation. Three times I have found them and I have been so mad that I threw them at once in the waste basket. They always come in an envelope similar to the kind Dr. S…'s notes come in. Somebody around the observatory must be sending them to me." The little fellow was quite sore and indignant about it and the other occupants of the car, <u>excluding</u> the embarrassed guilty party, offered various suggestions as to the identity of the guilty one.

One day last week the thermometer went up to 89.4 degrees! It is an all-time record for that day. Never before has so high a temperature been recorded on that particular day, and was it hot! When it gets as warm as that you really feel it in this humid climate. But since that day it has been very cool. That's the way the weather is here in Boston. One evening one can go out until 9 or 10 o'clock in his shirtsleeves and the next he needs an overcoat. Very fortunate it is that this weather changes so rapidly. Otherwise, it might at times become unbearable.

I want to tell you something I think is amusing. Friday evening I asked Lawrence to go with me for a walk around Fresh Pond, the little lake I have told you about before. About 10:30 I collected Lawrence at the observatory and we started off. All day the weather had been very unsettled, pouring down and clearing off alternately. When I first suggested to Lawrence that we go for a walk he questioned the wisdom of going very far on such an uncertain day. I said I thought it wouldn't rain - that a little rain wouldn't hurt us anyway, so he agreed, and later in the evening, as I have said, I collected him and we started on our walk.

Well, the evening was rather cool. In fact I had taken my gloves in order to keep my hands warm. I was wearing my old raincoat and no hat. Lawrence had a hat and a light zipper coat.

Fresh Pond is about a mile and half from here, and about three miles around. While we walked we noticed that the sky had become very dark and ominous. When we reached the lake I felt a few drops of water on my cheek, but we kept on. As we walked around the lake the breeze blew stronger. Presently flashes of lightning were seen. For some time we walked, while now and then lightening flashed. So far we had heard no thunder. By this time we were on the opposite side of the lake from home, and then lightening flashed and thunder rumbled around us, and in a few minutes rain was pouring down on us.

Fortunately, we were near a little shelter which was probably provided for golfers on the links beside the lake, so we ducked under the roof and listened to the thunder and watched the lightening until the rain lessened a little. Then we set out for home, me, holding my gloves on top of my head so that I wouldn't get my head soaked, and Lawrence muttering about being influenced against his better judgment to go walking so far on such a night. When we got home we dried ourselves and went to bed. Besides from getting a little wet our walk did us no harm.

For the present, mother dear, so long, and sweet dreams.

Your loving son, Harry.

May 8, 1938

Dear Mother,

I have a few moments to write to you as I am waiting for Lawrence to return so that we can go out and have dinner.

Yesterday the Observatory crowd had a picnic at Oak Ridge (22), the location of the Harvard Observing Station. Although the observatory has a number of telescopes here in Cambridge, their best and largest telescopes are out at the Ridge. Lawrence and I rode with Kay J…in her car. Leaving the Observatory at about 2 P.M., we arrived at the Ridge shortly after 3 o'clock. The ride was very nice. I rode in the rumble seat and got plenty of fresh air. En route to the Ridge we lost our way temporarily, but finally reached our destination after a few extra minutes of doubling back on our path.

Once there, we climbed the Fire tower on the hill. The man in charge was very agreeable and explained his duties to us. From his station we could see hills in New Hampshire. (People here on the East Coast call them mountains. Some of the peaks are over 5000 feet high, but they are not nearly as high as what we have in the West.) In the distance we could see signs of two fires.

For a couple of hours we played baseball. Not many of the players were expert, so I wasn't too ashamed of myself. Dr. S…, of whom I have written before, had never played baseball at all until a few days before this picnic. When he got up to bat he held the bat and swung it the way you would do if you were sweeping cobwebs from the ceiling. Before the game was over, he was hitting a pretty good average, however.

At about 6 o'clock we had an out-of-doors supper. Salad, hamburgers, hot dogs, tea, coffee, ice cream, cake, cookies - no wonder my tummy ached. On the way back to

Cambridge we stopped beside an apple tree to pick a few. It was about 9:30 when we arrived back home.

I must tell you about the observatory instruments. Miss J… and I - thanks to Lawrence - had a ride on an elevator arrangement in the building that houses the big 61 inch refracting telescope. This telescope is a marvelous instrument. The man in charge took us up and explained its operation briefly. Later, just before leaving, he set it on the planet Venus. Although it was not yet dark, and we couldn't see the planet with the naked eye, in this telescope it appeared to be a large, dazzling ball of fire. Dimly, to the side of Venus, we could see Mars, a reddish colored planet. This opportunity was more than Lawrence had expected. He said it was the first time he had ever looked through so large a telescope.

Well, it is now 7 o'clock and Lawrence hasn't returned. I am getting hungry. Maybe I will go off and have supper by myself.

May 9, 1938

This is Monday. Lawrence returned about 7:30 last night and we went to dinner. This morning I received your letter. I am sorry, but I am afraid that I won't be able to tell you for some time what I will be doing this summer. First of all, I have to do my best to secure a position. If nothing turns up, I may have to come home (the old man would like that) but I am going to at least make a good try at getting a job. Right now I am writing letters to various places. It may take me the best of today and the better part of the next couple of days to take care of this. After that I can only wait and hope. The way economic conditions are just at present it does not look hopeful, however.

In a day or two I will try to write again - when I have more time. Just now I want to try to see Professor Haertlein about the letters I am planning to send out.

I surely hope I can come home - at least for a visit - this summer. I have many things to tell you and I am sure that you have plenty to tell me.

Again, I send you my love, mother dear.

Your loving son, Harry

P.S. Don't worry about me. I will get some kind of job.

May 15, 1938

Dear Mother,

Today Lawrence, the Mink and I spent a couple of hours at the Harvard Arboretum, over in Boston (23). An Arboretum (I hope the spelling is correct) is a place where trees are cultivated for scientific and educational purposes. Near the entrance we saw pear trees - mostly from Asia - and various other kinds of trees. A bit further in were the lilacs - white lilacs, pink lilacs, deep, deep purple lilacs, big lilacs, tiny lilacs - there were every sort imaginable. Further along were the azaleas, which were very beautiful and delicate. Up on the hill were birches, ash, hickory, and pine trees. There were also white oaks and black oaks. I can't begin to name the kinds of trees in the arboretum. It is a very large place, covering hundreds of acres (maybe that's exaggerating a bit, but I think not) and probably containing thousands of different kinds of trees.

Today the weather has been unsettled as it has been for some time now. Lawrence and I are thankful that the weather hasn't been too hot and stuffy. Although many people prefer warm weather, we don't mind it being cool. Lawrence is up at the observatory, this being Sunday evening, but it has begun to rain, so he will probably be home in a short while.

It is now 10:45. After returning from Boston I began work on my research course. During the past several days I have done little else besides work on my report. In a couple of weeks examinations begin and I want to have this problem completed so that I can put all of my time into reviewing for the finals.

Your loving son,

Harry

May 16, 1938

Dear Mother,

Two of your letters just arrived. I have not yet mailed the letter I wrote yesterday evening, so I am adding a little bit more.

I am glad to hear that you have acquired a puppy for Johnny. He must like that very much. Poor little fellow, he must get lonely at times. Tell him that I said hello. In the letter are a couple of Harvard stickers for Johnny.

Today is another overcast day. Last night it rained, so Lawrence did not have to work. We slept until 10 minutes past nine this morning, so we both had plenty of sleep.

I have been writing to a number of people about work, and I think that I will land something - at least I hope so. Other years the fellows have had no trouble at all getting jobs, but it is a little different this year. There is no use worrying about what is going to happen, however. Dr. Casagrande has been writing to several outfits, recommending those of us who are going to be in need of a job, so we are hopeful. The Army Engineers think highly of Casagrande, and probably need some good engineers, so we may be working for the army before long. Junior Engineers get 2000 dollars per year.

Well mother dear I must get back to work, so I am going to mail this letter right now. So long, and remember, sweet dreams....

Harry

May 22, 1938

Dear Mother,

Again it is Sunday afternoon. Three more Sundays and this chapter of my life will be over - practically. The next week will mostly be spent listening to lectures and writing them up. The following week I will have to prepare for an examination that is to take place on June 3. After that, 10 days before another examination, then one the next day and it will all be over. The last two exams will be on the 13th and the 14th of June. But, this is Sunday afternoon. Lawrence and I have been out walking for a couple of hours, and will soon go down to the Wurst Haus (24) for supper. It has been a very lovely day.

Now it is nearly time for bed. C… C…, the boy in the room next to our room, is taking an examination tomorrow morning so he went to bed early. I do not want to disturb him, so I am writing, not typing, this letter.

Last Thursday I had an opportunity to visit a state that I had not yet been in - New Hampshire. Most of the boys in Soil Mechanics rode with Dr. Casagrande up to New Hampshire to see a demonstration of a method of determining the depth of rock or other hard material below the surface of the ground. We had an enjoyable ride, taking all afternoon for the trip. Our destination was just a few miles across the border from Massachusetts, so I have not been far into the State of New Hampshire.

Lawrence is over at the Observatory. I believe that the sky is sufficiently overcast so that he will not have to work all night. Probably he will be home in a short while. Next week he will be up nearly every night observing objects for his Thesis, so I hope he will be able to sleep tonight.

It is now past 11:30, so I believe I will go to bed. In the morning I will write a little more. Good-night.

Last Thursday evening Lawrence, the Mink, and I went over to Boston to hear the "Pops", which are just what the name says - popular concerts. The orchestra, about 85 members, is part of the regular Boston Symphony Orchestra. Every spring they play a series of concerts lasting through the months of May and June. They play selections from operas and orchestra numbers, and try to please everyone. Thursday's program was very good - thanks to Lawrence's excellent choice of a concert. We heard selections from Operas by Wagner; part of a symphony by Beethoven; Liszt's "Second Hungarian Rhapsody", a number by Ravel, "Wine, Woman, and Song, Waltzes" by Strauss, "Deep River" which was very fine, by Jacchia, a march, "Up the Street", by Morse, a couple of numbers by Mozart, and several others.

The "Pops" is an annual affair in Boston. Many people cannot afford to pay three or four dollars to hear a Symphony, and many folks would not enjoy a Symphony, even if they could afford it. To satisfy these people, they have the "Pops". The main floor of Symphony Hall is transformed into a glorified beer parlour. Here, one can have a seat for a dollar and can sit beside a table, sip champagne and listen to the strains of Moussorgasky's Hopak from "The Fair at Sorotchintzy" or a beautiful Rhapsody. Of course, the noise is terrific, but one doesn't mind noise in a beer parlour. If one wishes to enjoy the music, he can sit in either the first balcony, or in the second. The farther from the lower level one sits, the less he hears the noise. Up in the second balcony, which is an enormous distance up, one can watch the crowd from afar and really enjoy the concert - if one can call it a concert. That is what we did.

Anyway, Lawrence wouldn't pay more than 25 cents for the Mink. But, this week, he is planning to take Kay J…., the heiress, to the Pops, and for her he is willing to spend 50 cents for seats on the first balcony. But, for the Mink, 25 cents is all she is worth.

Friday evening I went to Boston with a boy who comes from Seattle and his girl-friend to hear Norman Thomas (25), the Socialist leader, speak. Dad might be interested in hearing about it. A couple of weeks previously, Thomas was driven out of New Jersey, so I was surprised to know that he would be allowed to speak in Boston, which is pretty strongly Republican.

We heard three excellent speeches. First, a minister presented a talk in which he proclaimed that war was not a tool that Jesus would have used or wanted his followers to use. (The meeting was a demonstration against war.) The second speaker, Miss Rankine (26), who was a Congresswoman at the time the United States went into the World War (27), pointed out that the United States has no reason in the world for maintaining a large Navy, or for spending a large amount of money in keeping up the Navy. Because of our geographic location we have nothing to fear with respect to attack from foreign countries. Thomas also presented an argument for keeping out of war. Although he is getting old, he is a very powerful, dynamic personality. I was glad of the opportunity of hearing him.

This coming Saturday, our group in Soil Mechanics is planning a trip down to Cape Cod, to investigate work that is being carried on down there. Among other things, we are to see dredging operations in action (28). We plan to leave Saturday morning at about 7 am from the dock, and to return Sunday noon. I will let you know how the trip turns out.

Your loving son, Harry

May 29, 1938

Dear Mother,

Yesterday Dr. Casagrande and the students in Soil Mechanics made an inspection trip out in Boston Harbor. We left Pierce Hall at 7:30 in the morning (those of us who rode with Dr. Casagrande), and met up with another group of students. We were all down at the U.S. Army Base (29) at 8:00 am. Because of fog the captain of the Josephine, the little boat that we were to go out on, delayed our start. While we were waiting for the fog to lift, Dr. Casagrande explained to us the work that had been done a couple of years ago to prevent the entire army base from collapsing into the ocean.

The Boston Army Base consists of a large area supported on a pile foundation off the shore of Boston. This area contains large warehouses, a power house, and various heavy buildings. It requires a good foundation, so when it was built large numbers of piles were driven deep into the clay below. A number of years after the base had been constructed, one could observe at low tide that all of the piles had been eaten away by pile worms until nothing but thin sticks remained. Obviously, something had to be done, and quickly, or the entire base would soon be dumped into the bay. To save the army base, a wall of steel sheet-piling was constructed around the entire area, and sand was pumped in until the piles were completely surrounded with sand. This procedure keeps the insects away from the piles, and prevents them from eating the piles further.

After about an hour, the fog began to clear, and we started out from the Army Base toward the Teledo 3, a dredge that is working in the harbour. A dredge is a monstrous floating machine. Not only does it have a large dipper similar to those on steam-shovels, but it contains all of the machinery necessary to operate the dredge, and means for providing for all of the men working on the dredge. It is really a ship. The dipper on this dredge could pick up 16 yards of clay in one scoop. The cable that pulls the dipper is over four inches in diameter.

After inspecting the Toledo 3 we went out to the drill boat, which drills holes in the rock where it is too close to the surface, so men can blast the rock loose. After the drill boat has done its damage, it passes on to some other spot. Finally the dredge removes the material with its big dipper and dumps it on barges which carry it out to deep water to be dumped. In spite of the fog, we were able to see the dredge and the drill boat, although they were not operating. We then returned to the Army Base and back to Pierce Hall.

Today B… F…, a young engineer from Checkoslovakia, dropped in on me. He is now employed by Prentice, White and Spencer, a contracting firm in New York. Early this year I agreed to make carbon copies of my notes in Soil Mechanics for him. He said he would pay me for doing it. All that was necessary to make copies for him was the insertion of a piece of carbon paper and an extra piece of paper. It required but a few moments of time, so it did not put me out much. Several days ago he wrote telling me that he was coming up to Cambridge. I told him that I would give him the notes that I had made during this semester and that I did not expect him to pay me for them. However, I told him that he might do me the favor of trying to get some papers on Foundation Engineering that I am interested in.

When he came, he brought me a copy of a very excellent book published by the company he now works for. This book is now out of print and cannot be purchased, so I am fortunate to be able to get a copy of it. My notes are of information that for the most part has not ever been published, so if he can read them, they should be of value to him. I'm glad I was able to do him this favor.

Tomorrow Fruehauf may take some friends up to Vermont. If he goes, he said he will reserve a place in his car for me. Perhaps I will be able to give you an account sometime later of a visit to the state of Vermont.

As yet I know nothing definite about jobs. Dr. Casagrande has written to a department of the U.S. Engineering office and something may come of this before long. Business seems to be pretty much in the dumps just now. It is a rather bad time to be trying to get a job. If I don't get something, I may have to come home - if dad will let me. On the other hand, if I should get a job, I may have to go directly from here to the job. Should I be so fortunate as to get a job I must not worry too much about other things that I would like to do.

I hope that you folks are making out all right and that you are still feeling well. So long as one is not sick in bed one has a lot to be thankful for!

Now it is 11:00 P.M. Lawrence is at the Observatory, waiting for the weather to make up its mind. This evening it was cloudy, but the sky cleared somewhat after dark. Since that time it has been rather undecided. Tomorrow is supposed to be a holiday, Memorial Day. Actually, for me it will be a day to get a lot of work done. I must do a lot of work before Friday, because I then have my first examination. Before that time I must finish reading a book, read a number of papers in the Proceedings (30), study several other papers and books, and study my notes. In addition I have a couple of problems to finish. Fortunately, I do not have to take the examination in Structures that most of my mates are taking.

This is Monday evening, and I have not yet mailed your letter. Sunday Lawrence and I went with Fruehauf up to Maine. We had a rather enjoyable trip, which I will explain later. So long now, and sweet dreams...

Your loving son, Harry

June 4, 1938

This evening it is raining like fury outside. Yesterday I took my first final examination and I will take the other two on the 13th and 14th of June. Lawrence is already preparing to leave. Today he bought his ticket and had a friend make out an itinerary for him. On the 11th he is planning to leave about 3 o'clock in the afternoon.

If my examinations ended earlier I might be able to ride home for nothing - in fact if I could take them early I could leave Wednesday, the 8th. A married couple is driving to Seattle and will take a couple of students without any charge - but I don't think I will be able to do it.

I believe I told you that I have been trying to get a job with the U.S. Army Engineer Office. This department needs men trained in Soil Mechanics, but because of Civil Service Requirements, ineligible men are not supposed to be hired as long as there are eligible men available who have passed the exams. Now, there are plenty of men waiting for jobs who have Civil Service ratings, but in the U. S. Engineer Office men are needed who have specialized training in Soil Mechanics. Very few men with this training are available, so competition is not too great.

Dr. Casagrande tells me that the office at Providence, Rhode Island could use a dozen men, but because of a lot of red tape, the man in charge cannot hire people. In previous years, this office has telegraphed at the last minute for men. When they want men, they generally want them quick. Dr. Casagrande has written to the man in charge of the Providence office, telling him of several of us who are anxious to get jobs. Nothing has happened yet, and nothing may happen for some time.

If I do not have a job when school is out on the 14th of June, I am going to start for home. First I am going to write to a number of people explaining why I must go home, and asking them to get in touch with me if they want me. Then I will go down to New York to talk with a number of influential engineers. From there, if nothing happens, I will start for "God's Country " and home. If I do not get a job immediately, something will very likely turn up before the summer is over. I would surely like to be able to spend a month or so at home this summer, so I am not going to worry too much about getting a job. Of course, I have got to get one in order to pay back what I have borrowed this year, if for no other reason, but a vacation would do no harm.

This is a favorite poem of a student at Wellesley College. I heard her say it at a meeting at the "Church around the corner on Mass Ave." and asked her to write it down for me. Here it is:

Isn't it strange that princes and kings
And clowns that caper in circus rings
And common folks like you and me
Are builders of eternity?

To each is given a set of rules,
An unshaped mass, a bag of tools
And each must make ere life has flown
A stumbling block, or a stepping stone.

Your loving son, Harry

June 11, 1938

Dear Folks,

Thank you all for your letters. I was very glad to hear from you. Dad, I want to thank you for your letter and Johnny, you are a smart little boy. Just keep up the good work. After this, if you don't get good grades, we'll know it's because you are loafing - so maybe you put yourself in a spot.

The other day I was talking with Glen Butterfield (31) and he suggested that if we got nothing else we might be able to get jobs at the University of Washington. In that case, it would not be in Soil Mechanics, but we will probably be lucky to get anything.

Although some folks would think time spent studying something you will never use is time wasted, I think this conclusion is wrong. In my mind it seems that a year such as I have spent studying under Dr. Casagrande here at Harvard should prove very valuable, whether I continue in Soil Mechanics or not. Of course it would be valuable more directly if I were to get a job in this field, but the contacts that I have made during the past year, the experience of being off by myself - away from my family, the opportunity to study under an outstanding scholar such as Dr. Casagrande - all these things should be worth much to me in my future life. No matter what I do for a living when I leave Cambridge, I will be better prepared than I would have been had I not come here.

I have written to several people, applying for work. In case one of them should offer me a position I suppose I will accept it. The likelihood of this possibility does not seem great, however. If nothing happens before Tuesday, June 14, I am planning to leave. Perhaps I will not leave until a few days after the 14th. At any rate, I intend to go by way of New York City, where I want to see a number of men who are very influential in the Engineering field. From there I will go West. Perhaps it would be just as well for me to go to Seattle, even if I should be offered a position here in the East. Professionally, I might not get so far by staying in the West, but there are other things to consider besides rank in one's profession.

Love, Harry

June 13, 1938

Dear Mother,

Your last letter arrived this morning. Please do not worry. I just want to tell you that very probably I will come home soon, but that if I do not, I will send you the money after a little while so that you can come visit me, wherever I am. In case I should get a job and would have to leave directly from here I will try as soon as possible to send you money for the railroad ticket. So don't worry about not seeing me again. Very probably you will be seeing too much of me.

I saw Lawrence off to California a few days ago. In some ways Lawrence is a strange person, but when I returned to my room I felt just a little bit funny inside. For a moment I realized how much one old friend from "back home" can do to keep one from feeling lonely. To be entirely friendless must be a terrible thing.

You asked me about Marion. I think I told you before that I have not been writing to her and that she has not been writing to me. This semester I wrote to her one time and she has written to me once. I guess I don't need to say any more.

I have been rather busy with my school work, but the other evening I went to the movies with a girl who is a student at Wellesley College. We went to a theater in Natick, a little town near Wellesley. After the show we got the last bus, so I could not see her to her door, but had to stay on the bus in order to get home. Other girls were going her way, so she was not alone. Perhaps I will never see her again. It was the only time I have taken her out. She is a rather nice young lady. Her home is in Illinois. Evidently her parents are pretty well off, because in the first place the cost of going to Wellesley is rather high, and in the second place this girl has been going home several times each year to see her folks. She also told of vacationing in Bermuda and going to California once every two years to visit relatives. Poor people do not make trips like that.

Did I tell you about the trip we made up into Maine? That is something I will have to tell you about when I see you. We did nothing exciting, only we can now say that we have been in one more state. While up in Maine we spent a few moments out on the "Rock-bound coast". We clambered out on the rocks and watched the surf pound wildly on the shore. The day was very calm, so the waves were not high. One time, as I recall, I did see fairly large waves on the Atlantic, but on the rest of the four or five times that I have been out to the coast it has been very calm.

Your loving son, Harry

PS There is going to be a conference at Harvard in a few days and I may stay for it. I will try to let you know what I am going to do as soon as I know. This conference lasts only a day or two.

No date - sent from Chicago
10112 Ewing Avenue
Chicago, Illinois

Dear Mother,

Tuesday evening I left Boston on the "Western Express" from South Station at 6:35 pm. Last evening the train pulled into Chicago at about 6 pm. A sort while later I telephoned Aunt Sofi and told her where I was. I hadn't told them I was coming so she was a bit surprised. She gave me directions and I found my way to their home here in South Chicago.

So, here I am again after nearly a year. I am planning to take the Great Northern Empire Builder out of Chicago this evening and I will arrive in Seattle Sunday morning, June 26, at 8:00 am train time. I believe that you don't have daylight savings time, so it will be 8:00 am. Western Standard Time (32). If that isn't too early to get up maybe you can come down to the depot. Perhaps it would be advisable to telephone the Great Northern Depot to make sure of the time the train arrives Sunday morning. There is one train every morning, but I should be on the one that pulls in Sunday morning. If I find that it will be different I will send a telegram en route.

I am riding in the coach, the same as I rode from Boston here to Chicago. On these particular trains, the coaches are very fine, having reclining seats, indirect lighting, and air-conditioning. The seat reclines far back and is very comfortable. Tuesday night I was a bit nervous so I slept poorly, but I believe that I will get enough sleep between here and Seattle. Last night I rested well, and I am being well fed while I am here, so I should be well prepared for the rest of the trip. The train leaves Chicago 11:15 tonight, so I will spend three nights on the train.

Sofi is going to give me a couple of canary birds to take home, so if they survive the trip you will have a couple of pets to care for. These birds are only about 2 ½ months old, are very tame, and the male bird sings some. It will be about 6 months before they are fully developed, however.

You might be interested in knowing that I passed all courses this semester, getting 2 A's, one A-, and one B+, so I will get my degree.

During the past year I lost about 15 pounds so I am a little thinner than before, but I am well, so I guess it does no real harm just being skinny. A month or so at home should help me to put on a little weight.

See you soon.

Harry

Notes by Number

1. Bill Shannon - friend from the State of Washington who gave Harry a job at Harvard.

2. Lawrence Aller - another friend who came to Harvard. They wound up rooming together the year (1937/38) Harry was there. He is currently (2002) Professor Emeritus at UCLA.

3. Dad - Henry Stockler, Harry's very kind stepfather.

4. Johnny - Harry's much younger half brother, born June 18, 1926.

5. The rooming house at 20 Mellen Street which was eventually purchased by Lesley College and has been used as one of their administrative buildings.

6. Elm trees – currently there are very few Elm trees in the Cambridge area. Most of them appear to have died off, probably from Dutch Elm disease which was rampant nation wide in the 1940s and 50s.

7. Museum of Fine Arts, Boston

8. Isabella Stewart Gardner Museum

9. Sander's theater in Cambridge. This was built as a memorial to Harvard students who died in the Civil War.

10. The "Coop" - Harvard Cooperative Society, which is a moderately priced store containing course books, art, music, basic clothing and other essentials needed for college life.

11. Fogg Art Museum – one of the many museums at Harvard University.

12. My dad continued to love football as long as I can remember. He was an avid fan of the Greenbay Packers in the 1950s, and when we lived in Stockton, California in the 1940s he frequently took me down the street to see games at the College of the Pacific (now called the University of the Pacific).

13. Harry returned to Seattle for a while after graduating and stayed with his mother and stepfather. He soon married my mother, Evelyn Noraine, was hired by the US. Army Corps of Engineers (as a civilian), and moved to Portland, Oregon. That is where I, his daughter, was born on December 17, 1941.

14. Gilbert Stuart (1755-1828) - Prolific early American Painter. He is most famous for his portraits of George Washington.

15. Joseph Mallord William Turner (1775-1851) - An English painter who did a lot of paintings of Venice. He used oils but his technique made them resemble watercolors.

16. John Singleton Copley (1738-1815) Early American portrait painter. Included in his subjects were John Hancock and Samuel and John Adams.

17. Dr. Menzel - Lawrence Aller's astronomy professor. Lawrence also worked for him as a teaching assistant at Radcliffe College.

18. Seattle Street is off of a short side street about a block from Cambridge Street in Allston. Currently it is a mixed residential and quasi industrial area. Warehouses, the Legal Seafoods fish market, and houses are all mixed together.

19. Lick Observatory on Mt. Hamilton in California. Owned by the University of California.

20. The Mount Auburn Cemetery in Cambridge, MA.

21. Massachusetts Institute of Technology

22. Oak Ridge Observatory - the large refracting telescope owned by Harvard University. It is in Harvard, Massachusetts, a few miles away from the university in Cambridge.

23. The Arnold Arboretum which is located in Jamaica Plain.

24. Restaurant in Harvard Square that is still there.

25. Norman Thomas (1884-1968) - socialist leader who ran for President of the United States on six different occasions. Born in Marion, Ohio, graduated from Princeton in 1905 and the Union Theological Seminary in 1911. He was a Presbyterian pastor and did settlement work in New York City.

26. Miss Rankin - former U.S. Congresswoman from Montana. Ardent pacifist and suffragette. Served two terms, 1917-1919 and 1941-1943. In 1917 refused to vote for war. In 1971 wrote to President Nixon urging him to end the Vietnam War.

27. My dad was obviously referring to WWI, but this letter was written in 1938, before WWII, so at that time WWI was simply referred to as the World War. It was supposed to be the "war to end all wars".

28. The Cape Cod Canal was widened and deepened by the digging of a channel under the Rivers and Harbors Act of 1935. The work was finished in 1940, just in time for WWII. ("Cape Cod Canal - Gateway to America's Intracoastal Waterway" U.S. Army Corps of Engineers, New England Division.)

29. There have been military bases in and around the Boston Harbor since the 1700s, so it is hard to know which one he was referring to. "Images of America, The Military History of Boston's Harbor Island." Gerald Butler, Arcadia Publishing, Charleston, South Carolina, 2000.

30. "Proceedings" are compiled for all major Engineering conferences and are made available for attendees, students and any interested persons. It is probable that he was doing a general search by subject of any relevant conferences.

31. Glen Butterfield - another friend from the University of Washington.

32. According to the website: webexhibits.org/daylightsaving/e.html: A law was passed in 1918 by the U.S. Congress to place the country on Daylight Saving Time for the duration of the war. In 1919 the law was repealed, but DST was continued in a few states (Massachusetts, Rhode Island) and a few cities (New York, Philadelphia, Chicago, etc.) It was later reinstated nation wide during WWII. Thus Boston and Chicago were on Daylight Savings Time when Harry was there, but Seattle and the State of Washington were not.

Photos of Cambridge

A scene in the yard, Harvard College

Harvard Yard

Harvard Square with the Harvard Yard on the right. Subway entrance just behind the young lady on the right.

Memorial Chapel, in memory of the World War. In Harvard College Yard.

Civil War Memorial, built to honor Harvard students and alumni who died in the American Civil War.

Harvard College Observatory in winter.

Statue in Cambridge of a Minute Man.

Office Building, Harvard College Observatory. (Note the ivy covered buildings, hence the name "Ivy League." The ivy has since been removed as the roots were pulling the bricks and mortar apart!)

20 Mellen Street with the Elm tree where the birds sat and chirped in the mornings.

Looking along Mellen Street

The Charles River in winter showing the Harvard buildings in the background and the Harvard boat house on the water.

Harry Cedergren on the North Shore, Atlantic Sea-Coast, near Lynn, MA,
Thanksgiving Day, November 25, 1937.